THE BOOK OF

LULLABIES

Wonderful songs and rhymes passed down from generation to generation

Compiled by John M. Feierabend

GIA FIRST STEPS · CHICAGO

Compiled by
John M. Feierabend

Artwork: Diana Appleton
Design: Nina Fox

GIA First Steps is an imprint of
GIA Publications, Inc.

ISBN: 1-57999-056-8
G-4979

Once upon a time, parents (and grandparents) soothed and amused their babies with songs that were sung to them when they were children. As those babies grew up and became parents, they would sing those same tunes to their children. In this way, wonderful songs and rhymes would be passed on orally, linking one generation to another through shared memories of comfort and joy.

Families today are more rushed and more geographically dispersed than ever before. Our cherished songs and rhymes, many of them hundreds of years old, are gradually being forgotten. They are being replaced by market-driven ear candy, tunes that may provide a temporary rush but exist mostly to help sell this year's hot new toys or trends.

The *First Steps in Music* series of books and recordings is an attempt to preserve the rich repertoire of traditional and folk literature; to enable today's families to remember and to learn songs and rhymes that have inspired wonder and joy in children for generations.

The lullabies in this book have been gathered over the past twenty years. Many of the most interesting examples, not readily available in print elsewhere, were collected from the elderly, who often recalled songs and/or rhymes with great affection reminding them of loving moments they had shared with young people in the past.

Some scholars believe that the lullaby is the root, the genesis, of all sung music. Lullabies are certainly one of the loveliest ways of showing a child how deeply you feel for him or her. Long before babies develop the ability to understand the lyrics, they are calmed, reassured and comforted by these songs, especially when, after several repetitions of the lullaby, the tune is hummed.

It is my hope that the collections of songs and rhymes presented in this series will help parents and other loving adults comfort and inspire wonder in children for generations to come.

John M. Feierabend

How to Sing Lullabies

Sit on the floor or in a chair and cradle baby in your arms.
Rock back and forth or from side to side keeping time with the
song. Gently tap on baby's back while rocking back and forth.
Or, with the help of a friend, lay baby on a towel or small
blanket. Each of you take an end of the towel or blanket and

rock child on floor

rock child in chair

have the child rock

gently sway baby back and forth while singing a lullaby. After
several repetitions of the lullaby, end by humming the tune.
This will heighten the mood of "hushed wonder." When baby
is old enough to hold a stuffed animal, sing lullabies for your
child while he or she rocks "baby" back and forth.

About Lullabies

Every culture, whether primitive or sophisticated, shares
lullabies with its babies. Lullabies emerge out of a need to
express something deeper than words alone can express.
Because lullabies communicate as much below the surface as
they do on the surface, they are among the most expressive
examples of music known and one of the most wonderful ways
to communicate your love and affection to your baby. Lullabies
plant the seeds for lifelong musical sensitivities. Lucky is the
child fortunate enough to have been loved with lullabies.

LULLABIES

Aija, Ancīt, Aija (Lullaby My Jamie) *Latvian*

Ai - ja, An - cīt, Ai - ja,   Sal - dā mied - zi -
Lull - a - by   my Jam - ie,   Soft - ly sleep   my

ņā,   Mā - siņ te - vi šu - pos,
child,   Sis - ter rocks   you gent - ly,

Vieg - lām ro - ci - ņām.
Soft   her hands   and mild.

Verse

Aija, Ancīt, Aija,
Saldā miedziņā,
Māsiņ tevi šūpos,
Vieglām rociņām.

Translation:

Lullaby my Jamie,
Softly sleep my child,
Sister rocks you gently,
Soft her hands and mild.

A La Puerta del Cielo *Spanish*

A la puer-ta del cie-lo ven - den za - pa - tos,

Para los an - gel - i - tos que en - tran des - cal - zos,

Duér - me - te, ni - ño, duér - me - te, ni - ño,

Duér - me - te, ni - ño, ar - ru, ar - ru.

Verse 1

A la puerta del cielo venden zapatos,
Para los angelitos que entran descalzos,
Duérmete, niño, duérmete, niño,
Duérmete, niño, arru, arru.

Verse 2

A los niños que duermen Dios los bendice,
A las madres que velan Dios las asiste,
Duérmete, niño, duérmete, niño,
Duérmete, niño, arru, arru.

General Translation:

Verse 1
In heaven there are shoes for
  barefoot angels,
Sleep, baby, sleep.

Verse 2
God will watch over the sleeping
  children and their mothers.
Sleep, baby, sleep.

All Me Rock, Me Rock Boysie *Caribbean*

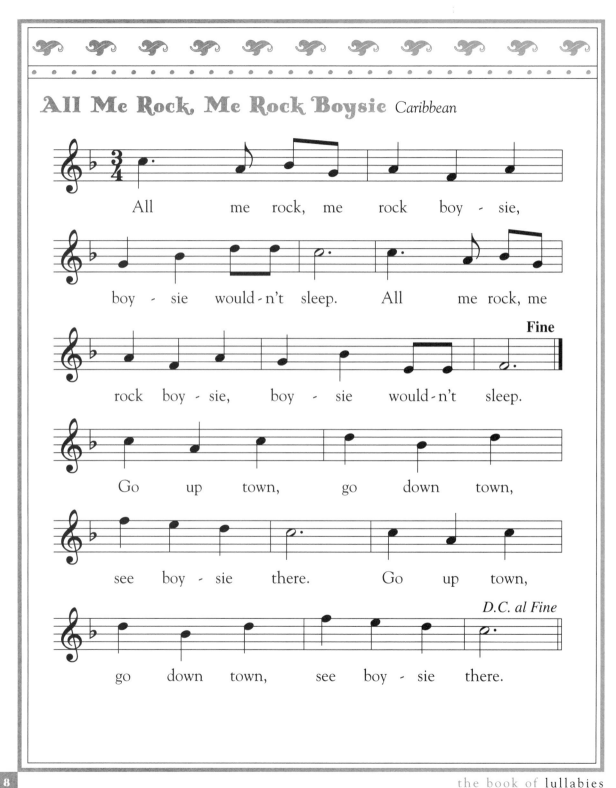

Verse

All me rock, me rock boysie, boysie wouldn't sleep.
All me rock, me rock boysie, boysie wouldn't sleep.
Go up town, go down town, see boysie there.
Go up town, go down town, see boysie there.
All me rock, me rock boysie, boysie wouldn't sleep.
All me rock, me rock boysie, boysie wouldn't sleep.

All the Pretty Little Horses

Hush-a-bye, don't you cry, Go to sleep lit-tle ba - by. When you wake you shall have, All the pret-ty lit-tle hors-es. Blacks and bays, dap-ples and grays, All the pret-ty lit-tle hors-es. Hush-a-bye, don't you cry, Go to sleep lit-tle ba-by.

Verse

Hush-a-bye, don't you cry,
Go to sleep little baby.
When you wake you shall have,
All the pretty little horses.
Blacks and bays, dapples and grays,
All the pretty little horses.
Hush-a-bye, don't you cry,
Go to sleep little baby.

Ally Bally

Al - ly bal - ly, al -ly bal-ly bee, Sit-tin' on your

dad-dy's knee. Want -in' for a wee pen - ny To

buy some choc - 'late can - dy.

Verse 1

Ally bally, ally bally bee,
Sittin' on your daddy's knee.
Wantin' for a wee penny
To buy some choc'late candy.

Verse 2

Ah, poor thing you're gettin' very thin,
A bundle of bones all covered with skin.
Now you're gettin' a wee double chin
From all that choc'late candy.

Verse 3

Go to sleep now, my little one,
Seven o'clock and your playing's done.
Open your eyes to the morning sun,
I'll give you some choc'late candy.

All Through the Night

Sleep, my child, and peace at-tend thee, all through the

night. Guard - ian an - gels God will send thee,

all through the night. Soft the drows - y

hours are creep - ing, hill and vale in slum - ber steep - ing,

I, my lov - ing vig - il keep - ing, all through the night.

Verse 1

Sleep, my child, and peace attend
  thee, all through the night.
Guardian angels God will send thee,
  all through the night.
Soft the drowsy hours are creeping,
  hill and vale in slumber steeping,
I, my loving vigil keeping,
  all through the night.

Verse 2

While the moon her watch is keeping,
  all through the night.
While the weary world is sleeping,
  all through the night,
O'er thy spirit gently stealing,
  visions of delight revealing,
Breathes a pure and holy feeling,
  all through the night.

Arrorró, mi Niño *South American: Spanish*

A - rro - rró, mi ni - ño, a - rro - rró, mi sol,

A - rro - rró, pe - da - zo de mi co - ra - zón.

Verse 1

Arrorró, mi niño, arrorró, mi sol,
Arrorró, pedazo de mi corazón.

Verse 2

Señora Santa Ana, Señor San Joaquín,
Haranlá la cama en el toronjil.

Verse 3

Y por cabecera pónganle un jazmín,
Para que se duerma como un sera.

General Translation:

Verse 1
Hush-a-bye my baby,
  hush-a-bye my sun;
Hush-a-bye, part of my heart.
Verse 2
St. Anne and St. Joachim,
  make up the cradle
In a bed of lemon balm.
Verse 3
And for a pillow,
  put a jasmine plant,
So the baby will sleep
  like an angel.

Ayle Lyu Lye, Lyu Lye *Yiddish*

Ay - le lyu lye, lyu lye, Schlof - zhe schlof mayn g'du - le,

Mach - zhe tsu day - ne ey - ge - lekh di fay - ne.

Verse

Ayle lyu lye, lyu lye,
Schlofzhe schlof mayn g'dule,
Machzhe tsu dayne eygelekh di fayne.

General Translation:

Sleep my precious baby.
Close your pretty eyes.

Baby Dear, Baby Dear, Don't You Cry

Ba - by dear,   ba - by dear,   don't   you   cry.

Fa - ther will   come   to   you   by   and   by.

Moth - er   is   bak - ing you   cakes   to   eat.

Verse

Baby dear, baby dear, don't you cry.
Father will come to you by and by.
Mother is baking you cakes to eat.

Baloo Baleerie *Gaelic*

Ba - loo ba - lee - rie, Ba -
loo ba - lee - rie, Ba - loo ba -
lee - rie, Ba - loo ba - lee. Go a -
way, lit - tle fair - ies, Go a -
way, lit - tle fair - ies, Go a - way, lit-tle
fair - ies, From our small room.

Verse

Baloo baleerie,   Go away, little fairies,
Baloo baleerie,   Go away, little fairies,
Baloo baleerie,   Go away, little fairies,
Baloo balee.   From our small room.

Bed Is Too Small

Bed is too small for my tir - ed - ness;

Give me a hill - side with trees.

Tuck a cloud up un - der my chin.

Lord, blow the moon out, please.

Verse 1

Bed is too small for my tiredness;
Give me a hillside with trees.
Tuck a cloud up under my chin.
Lord, blow the moon out, please.

Verse 2

Rock me to sleep in a cradle of dreams;
Sing me a lullaby of dreams.
Tuck a cloud up under my chin.
Lord, blow the moon out, please.

Bim Bam, Biri, Biri, Bam *Yiddish*

Bim bam, bi-ri, bi-ri, bam. Bi-ri, bi-ri bim bam,

bi-ri, bi-ri, bam. Bim bam, bim bam,

bim bam, bi-ri, bi-ri, bam. Bim bam,

bim bam, bim bam, bi-ri, bi-ri, bam.

Verse

Bim bam, biri, biri, bam.
Biri, biri bim bam, biri, biri, bam.
Bim bam, bim bam, bim bam, biri, biri, bam.
Bim bam, bim bam, bim bam, biri, biri, bam.

Brahms' Lullaby (Lullaby and Good Night)

German, Johannes Brahms, Fritz Simrock, Lyrics

Gu - ten A - bend, gut' Nacht, Mit Ro - sen be -
Lull - a - by and good night, with ros - es de -

dacht, Mit Näg - lein be - steckt, Schlüpf'
light, With lil - ies be - decked is

un - ter die Deck. Mor - gen früh, wenn Gott
ba - by's wee bed. Lay thee down now and

will, Wirst du wie - der ge - weckt; Mor - gan
rest, may thy slum - ber be blest; Lay thee

früh, wenn Gott will, Wirst du wie - der ge - weckt.
down now and rest, may thy slum - ber be blest.

Verse

Guten Abend, gut' Nacht,
Mit Rosen bedacht,
Mit Näglein besteckt,
Schlüpf' unter die Deck.
Morgen früh, wenn Gott will,
Wirst du wieder geweckt;
Morgan früh, wenn Gott will,
Wirst du wieder geweckt.

Translation:

Lullaby and good night,
  with roses delight,
With lilies bedecked is baby's wee bed.
Lay thee down now and rest,
  may thy slumber be blest;
Lay thee down now and rest,
  may thy slumber be blest.

Variation

Lullaby and good night,
  in the soft evening light,
Like a rose in its bed,
  lay down your sweet head.
When morning is near,
  I will wake you, my dear.
When morning is near,
  I will wake you, my dear.

Bye, Baby Bunting

Bye, ba - by bunt - ing. Dad - dy's gone a

hunt - ing, To catch a lit - tle rab - bit skin To

wrap his ba - by bunt - ing in.

Verse

Bye, baby bunting.
Daddy's gone a hunting,
To catch a little rabbit skin
To wrap his baby bunting in.

Bye, My Baby, Bye

Bye, my ba-by, bye. Bye, my ba-by,

bye. Mom - ma's gone to the mail - boat.

Mom - ma's gone to the mail - boat, bye.

Verse 1

Bye, my baby, bye.
Bye, my baby, bye.
Momma's gone to the mailboat.
Momma's gone to the mailboat, bye.

Verse 2

Bye, my baby, bye.
Bye, my baby, bye.
Daddy's gone to the mailboat.
Daddy's gone to the mailboat, bye.

Verse 3

Sleep, my baby, go to sleep.
Sleep, my baby, sleep.
Momma's back from the mailboat.
Daddy's back, too, from the mailboat, bye.

Bye'n Bye, Bye'n Bye

Bye'n bye, bye'n bye, Stars shin - ing
Stars shin - ing
Stars shin - ing

num - ber, num - ber one, num-ber two, num-ber three, Good
num - ber, num - ber four, num-ber five, num-ber six,
num - ber, num - ber sev'n, num-ber eight, num-ber nine,

Lord, bye 'n bye, bye 'n bye, Good Lord, bye 'n bye.

Verse 1

Bye'n bye, bye'n bye,
Stars shining number, number one,
  number two, number three,
Good Lord, bye'n bye, bye'n bye,
Good Lord, bye'n bye.

Verse 2

Bye'n bye, bye'n bye,
Stars shining number, number four,
  number five, number six,

Good Lord, bye'n bye, bye'n bye,
Good Lord, bye'n bye.

Verse 3

Bye'n bye, bye'n bye,
Stars shining number, number sev'n,
  number eight, number nine,
Good Lord, bye'n bye, bye'n bye,
Good Lord, bye'n bye.

Bye, Bye Baby, Baby Bye

Bye,   bye   ba - by,   ba - by   bye.

My   lit - tle   ba - by,   ba - by   bye.

Verse

Bye, bye baby, baby bye.
My little baby, baby bye.

Bye-o, Bye-o, Bye-o Baby

Bye-o, bye - o, bye-o ba - by, Close your

lit - tle ba-by eyes. You are mom - my's lit-tle

ba - by, You are dad - dy's lit-tle prize.

Verse

Bye-o, bye-o, bye-o baby,
Close your little baby eyes.
You are mommy's little baby,
You are daddy's little prize.

Bye-o, My Baby, Baby Bye-o, Bye

Bye - o, my ba - by, ba - by bye - o, bye,

Go to sleep my hon - ey, hon - ey bye - o, bye.

Bye - o, my sug - ar, sug - ar go to sleep,

You are a hon - ey, hon - ey bye - o, bye.

Verse

Bye-o, my baby, baby bye-o, bye,
Go to sleep my honey, honey bye-o, bye.
Bye-o, my sugar, sugar go to sleep,
You are a honey, honey bye-o, bye.

Cherries Are Ripe

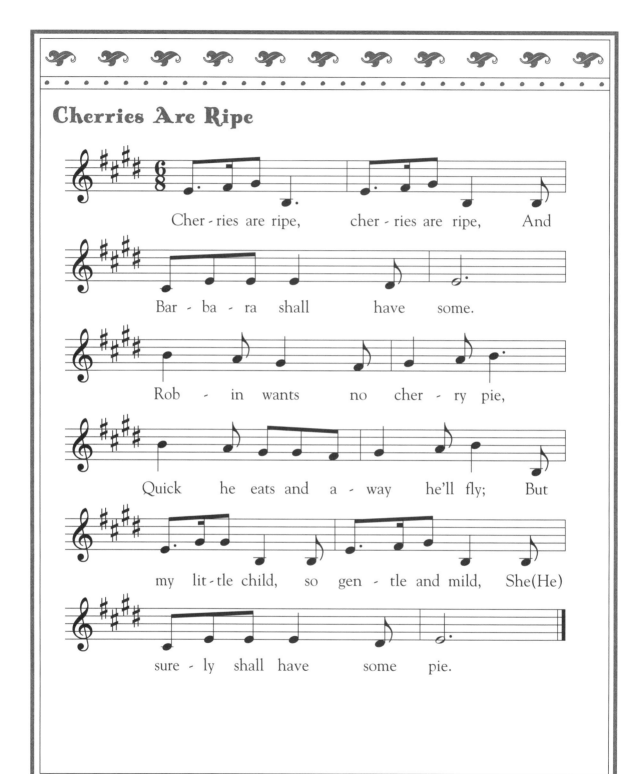

Cher - ries are ripe, cher - ries are ripe, And

Bar - ba - ra shall have some.

Rob - in wants no cher - ry pie,

Quick he eats and a - way he'll fly; But

my lit - tle child, so gen - tle and mild, She(He)

sure - ly shall have some pie.

Verse

Cherries are ripe, cherries are ripe,
And Barbara shall have some.
Robin wants no cherry pie,
Quick he eats and away he'll fly;
But my little child, so gentle and mild,
She(He) surely shall have some pie.

Detta, Detta, Please Be Nice *Japanese*

Det - ta,   det - ta,   please   be   nice,

If you see a   rab-bit who is   pound-ing   up   the   rice.

When   he   makes   a   cake   we'll   have   a   slice.

Verse

Detta, detta, please be nice,
If you see a rabbit who is
  pounding up the rice.
When he makes a cake
  we'll have a slice.

Dodo, L'enfant Dors (Sleep, Baby Sleep) *Belgian*

Do - do, l'en - fant dors, l'en - fant dor - mi -
Sleep, ba - by sleep, ba - by go to

ra bien vi - te. Do - do, l'en - fant dors,
sleep quite quick - ly. Sleep, ba - by sleep,

l'en - fant dor - mi - ra bien - tot. Do - do,
ba - by go to sleep at once. Sleep,

l'en - fant dors, l'en - fant dor - mi - ra bien vi - te.
ba - by sleep, ba - by go to sleep quite quick - ly.

Mm mm mm mm mm mm mm mm mm mm mm mm.

Verse

Dodo, l'enfant dors,
  l'enfant dormira bien vite.
Dodo, l'enfant dors,
  l'enfant dormira bientot.
Dodo, l'enfant dors,
  l'enfant dormira bien vite.
Mm mm mm.

Translation:

Sleep, baby sleep,
  baby go to sleep quite quickly.
Sleep, baby sleep,
  baby go to sleep at once.
Sleep, baby sleep,
  baby go to sleep quite quickly.
Mm mm mm.

Dors, Dors (Sleep, Sleep) *Cajun*

Dors, dors, 'ti bé - bé,

(é)'cout-es la ri - viè - re, (é)'cout-es la ri - viè - re,

Dors, dors, 'ti bé - bé,

(é)'cout - es la ri - viè - re cou - ler.

Verse

Dors, dors, 'ti bébé,
  é'coutes la rivière, é'coutes la rivière,
Dors, dors, 'ti bébé,
  é'coutes la rivière couler.

Translation:

Sleep, sleep little babe, listen to
  the river, listen to the river,
Sleep, sleep little babe, listen to
  the river running.

Duerme, Duerme, Muñequita *Spanish*

Duer - me, duer - me,   mu - ñe - qui - ta,   duer - me   ya.

Si   tu   duer - mes   tu   ma - mi - ta   dor - mir - á.

Verse

Duerme, duerme, muñequita, duerme ya.
Si tu duermes tu mamita dormirá.

General Translation:

Sleep, sleep, my little one,
  go to sleep now.
If you sleep your mama
  will sleep too.

Duerme Pronto, Niño Mío
(Go to Sleep, My Little Baby) *Spanish*

Duer - me pron - to, ni - ño mi - o,
Go to sleep, my lit - tle ba - by,

duer - me pron - to sin llo - rar,
go to sleep and do not cry.

Que es - tás en los bra - zos de tu
Moth - er's arms will hold you gen - tly

ma - dre que te va a can - tar.
while she sings a lull - a - by.

Verse

Duerme pronto, niño mío,
  duerme pronto sin llorar.
Que estás en los brazos de tu madre
  que te va a cantar.

Translation:

  Go to sleep, my little baby,
  go to sleep and do not cry.
  Mother's arms will hold you
  gently while she sings a lullaby.

Duérmete Mí Niño, Duérmete Mí Amor *Mexican*

Duér - me - te mí ni - ño, duér - me - te mí a - mor.

Duér - me - te pe - da - zo de mí co - ra - zón.

Es - te ni - ño lin - do que na - cío de

no - che, Qui - ere que lo lle - ven

1. a pa - sear en co - che.

2. a pa - sear en co - che.

Verse

Duérmete mí niño, duérmete mí amor.
Duérmete pedazo de mí corazón.
Este niño lindo que nació de noche,
Quiere que lo lleven a pasear en coche.

General Translation:

Sleep my little boy, sleep my love.
Sleep little morsel of my heart.
This beautiful boy
  who was born at night,
He wants to go for a ride in the car.

Duérmete Niño Bonito *Spanish*

Duér - me - te ni - ño bo - ni - to, La la

la la la la la la la la la, Duér - me -

te mi a - mor con es - ta can - ción. Yo es - toy

jun - to a ti, duér - me - te.

Verse

Duérmete niño bonito,
La la la la la la la la la la la,
Duérmete mi amor con esta canción.
Yo estoy junto a ti, duérmete.

General Translation:

Go to sleep, my pretty baby.
La la la la la la la la la la la,
Go to sleep my love with this song.
I am together with you,
go to sleep.

Fais Dodo, Colas mon P'tit Frère
(Sleep, My Little Brother) *Cajun*

Fais do - do, Co - las mon p'tit frè - re
Sleep, my lit - tle broth - er.

fais do - do, tu auras du lo - lo.
Sleep, and you will have some-thing to drink.

Verse

Fais dodo, Colas mon p'tit frère.
Fais dodo, tu auras du lolo.

Translation:

Sleep, my little brother.
Sleep, and you will have something
to drink.

Fais Dodo, mon Pétit Bébé *Cajun*

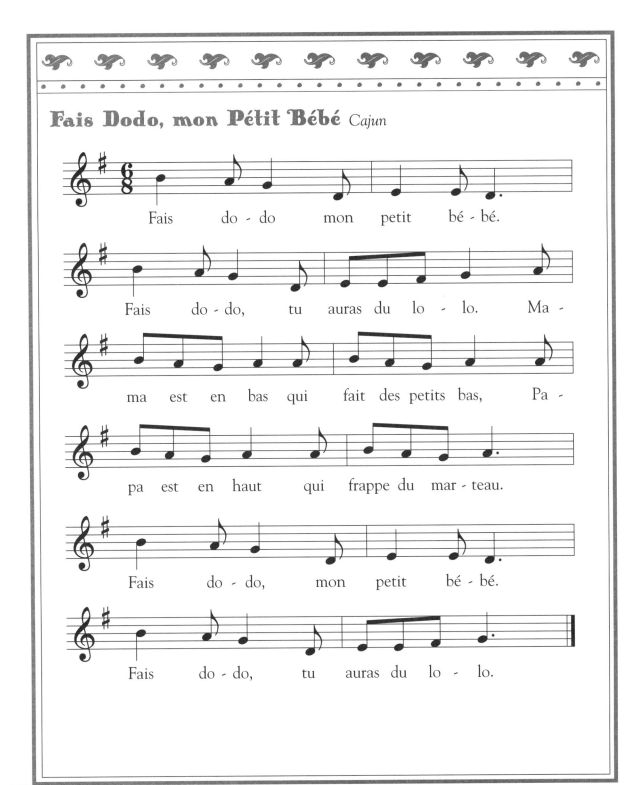

Fais do - do mon petit bé - bé.

Fais do - do, tu auras du lo - lo. Ma -

ma est en bas qui fait des petits bas, Pa -

pa est en haut qui frappe du mar - teau.

Fais do - do, mon petit bé - bé.

Fais do - do, tu auras du lo - lo.

Verse

Fais dodo, mon petit bébé.
Fais dodo, tu auras du lolo.
Mama est en bas qui fait des petits bas,
Papa est en haut qui frappe du
  marteau.
Fais dodo, mon petit bébé.
Fais dodo, tu auras du lolo.

Translation:

Sleep, my little baby, sleep.
Sleep, and you will have
  something to drink.
Mama is downstairs and she's
  making little socks,
Papa is upstairs and he's hitting
  the hammer.
Sleep, my little baby, sleep.
Sleep, and you will have some-
  thing to drink.

Golden Slumbers

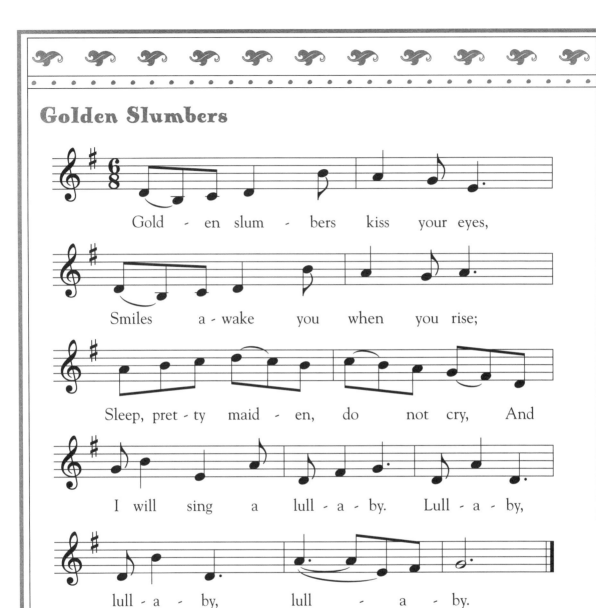

Gold - en slum - bers kiss your eyes,

Smiles a - wake you when you rise;

Sleep, pret - ty maid - en, do not cry, And

I will sing a lull - a - by. Lull - a - by,

lull - a - by, lull - a - by.

Verse 1

Golden slumbers kiss your eyes,
Smiles awake you when you rise;
Sleep, pretty maiden, do not cry,
And I will sing a lullaby.
Lullaby, lullaby, lullaby.

Verse 2

Care you know not, therefore sleep
While I o'er you watch do keep;
Sleep, pretty darling, do not cry,
And I will sing a lullaby.
Lullaby, lullaby, lullaby.

Go to Sleep, Go to Sleepy

Verse

Go to sleep, go to sleepy,
Go to sleepy little baby.
Hush li'l baby and don't you cry,
Go to sleepy little baby.

Mom and papa have gone to town,
Buy a pretty little pony.
Go to sleep, go to sleepy,
Go to sleepy little baby.

Go to Sleep My Darling Baby (Babushka Baio)

Russian

Go to sleep my dar-ling ba-by, Ba-bush-ka ba - io.

See the moon is shin-ing on you, Ba-bush-ka ba - io.

Verse 1

Go to sleep my darling baby,
Babushka baio.
See the moon is shining on you,
Babushka baio.

Verse 2

I will tell you many stories
If you close your eyes.
Go to sleep my darling baby,
Babushka baio.

Great Big Dog

Great big dog came down the mea - dow.

Wagged his tail and shook the mead - ow.

Go 'way dog, go 'way dog.

You can't have my ba - by.

Verse

Great big dog came down the meadow.
Wagged his tail and shook the meadow.
Go 'way dog, go 'way dog.
You can't have my baby.

Gute Nacht, Gut' Nacht, Mein Feines Lieb
(Good Night, Good Night, My Dear Sweetheart) *German*

Gu-te Nacht, gut' Nacht, mein fei - nes Lieb,

Gu-te Nacht, schlaf' wohl, mein Kind. Gu - te

Nacht, gut' Nacht, mein fei - nes Lieb, Gu - te

Nacht, schlaf' wohl, mein Kind. Dass dich die En - gel

hü - ten all', Die in dem schön - en

Him - mel sind. Gu-te Nacht, gut' Nacht, mein

fei - nes Lieb, Schlaf' wohl, schlaf' wohl, mein Kind!

Verse

Gute Nacht, gut' Nacht,
  mein feines Lieb,
Gute Nacht, schlaf' wohl, mein Kind.
Gute Nacht, gut' Nacht,
  mein feines Lieb,
Gute Nacht, schlaf' wohl, mein Kind.
Dass dich die Engel hüten all',
Die in dem schönen Himmel sind.
Gute Nacht, gut' Nacht,
  mein feines Lieb,
Schlaf' wohl, schlaf' wohl, mein Kind!

Translation:

Good night, good night,
  my dear sweetheart,
Good night, sleep well, my child.
Good night, good night,
  my dear sweetheart,
Good night, sleep well, my child.
For the angels will take care of you,
The angels that are
  in beautiful heaven.
Good night, good night,
  my dear sweetheart,
Sleep well, sleep well, my child!

Guéqué Solingaie *Louisiana: French Creole*

Gué - qué so-lin-gaie, Ba - li chi-min lá. Ma di

li, oui ma di li. Cale-basse li con-nin par -

ler! Cale-basse li con-nin par - ler!

Verse 1

Guéqué solingaie,
Bali chimin lá,
Ma di li, oui ma di li.
Calebasse li connin parler!
Calebasse li connin parler!

Verse 2

Guéqué solingaie,
Bali chimin lá,
Ma di li, oui ma di li.
Cocodril li connin chanter!
Cocodril li connin chanter!

Verse 3

Guéqué solingaie,
Bali chimin lá,
Ma di li, oui ma di li.
Tichou li connin trangler!
Tichou li connin trangler!

Translation:

Verse 1
Look at my baby Solingaie,
Clear the way for him.
I will tell him, yes I will tell him.
His little drum knows how to talk!
His little drum knows how to talk!

Verse 2
Look at my baby Solingaie,
Clear the way for him.
I will tell him, yes I will tell him.
His little bird knows how to sing!
His little bird knows how to sing!

Verse 3
Look at my baby Solingaie,
Clear the way for him.
I will tell him, yes I will tell him.
My little darling, he knows how to cry!
My little darling, he knows how to cry!

Huna Blentyn (Suo Gan) (Sleep, My Baby) *Welsh*

Hun - a blen-tyn, yn fy myn-wes, Clud a chyn-nes
Sleep, my ba - by, rest, my loved one, Soft - ly slum-ber

yd - y hon. Breich - iau mam syn dyn am-dan-at,
now with me. Clasped in moth-er's arms so ten-der,

Car - iad mam sy dan fy mron. Ni chaiff dim am -
Warm in moth-er's love for thee. Naught shall ev - er

har - uth gyn - tun, Ni wna un-dyn a thi gam;
come to harm thee While my lov-ing watch I keep;

Hun - a'n daw-el an - nwyl blen - tyn
Thou, my pret-ty one, shall slum - ber

Hun - a'n dwym ar fron dy fam.
While I sing thy lull - a - by.

Verse

Huna blentyn yn fy mynwes,
Clud a chynnes ydy hon.
Breichiau mam syn dyn amdanat,
Cariad mam sy dan fy mron.
Ni chaiff dim amharuth gyntun,
Ni wna undyn a thi gam,
Huna'n dawel annwyl blentyn
Huna'n dwym ar fron dy fam

Translation:

Verse 1
Sleep, my baby, rest, my loved one,
Softly slumber now with me.
Clasped in mother's arms so tender,
Warm in mother's love for thee.
Naught shall ever come to harm thee
While my loving watch I keep;
Thou, my pretty one, shall slumber
While I sing thy lullaby.
Verse 2
Sleep, my baby, on my bosom,
Warm and cozy it will prove.
Round you mother's arms are folding,
In her heart, a mother's love.
There shall no one come to harm you,
Nothing ever break your rest;
Sleep, my darling babe in quiet,
Sleep on mother's gentle breast.
Verse 3
Sleep, my baby, rest, my loved one,
While the evening shadows creep.
Why, my dearest, art thou smiling,
Smiling sweetly in thy sleep?
Can it be that all the angels
In God's Heaven smile on thee?
Rest, my darling, smile and slumber
While I sing thy lullaby.

Hush, My Baby, Don't You Cry

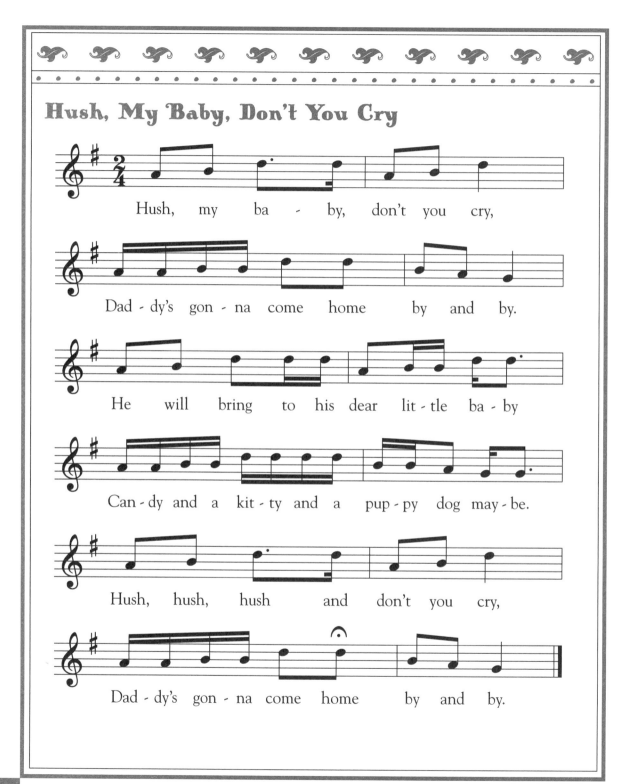

Hush, my ba - by, don't you cry,

Dad - dy's gon - na come home by and by.

He will bring to his dear lit - tle ba - by

Can - dy and a kit - ty and a pup - py dog may - be.

Hush, hush, hush and don't you cry,

Dad - dy's gon - na come home by and by.

Verse

Hush, my baby, don't you cry,
Daddy's gonna come home by and by.
He will bring to his dear little baby
Candy and a kitty and a puppy dog maybe.
Hush, hush, hush and don't you cry,
Daddy's gonna come home by and by.

Hush, Little Baby, Don't Say a Word

Hush, lit - tle ba - by, don't say a word,

Pa - pa's gon - na buy you a mock - ing bird.

Verse 1

Hush, little baby, don't say a word,
Papa's gonna buy you a mockingbird.

Verse 2

If that mockingbird don't sing,
Papa's gonna buy you a diamond ring.

Verse 3

If that diamond ring turns brass,
Papa's gonna buy you a looking glass.

Verse 4

If that looking glass gets broke,
Papa's gonna buy you a billy goat.

Verse 5

If that billy goat won't pull,
Papa's gonna buy you a cart and bull.

Verse 6

If that cart and bull turn over,
Papa's gonna buy you a dog named Rover.

Verse 7

If that dog named Rover won't bark,
Papa's gonna buy you a horse and cart.

Verse 8

If that horse and cart fall down,
You'll still be the sweetest
little baby in town.

Hush, My Babe, Lie Still and Slumber (Variation 1)

Hush, my babe, lie still and slum - ber,

Ho - ly an - gels guard thy bed.

Heav'n - ly bless - ings with - out num - ber,

Gen - tly steal - ing on thy head.

A note about Hush, My Babe, Lie Still and Slumber:

True to the nature of folk music, variation is an expected characteristic. Sometimes the variation is in the form of varied words with the same melody and sometimes it is the reverse, as is the case in the following three lullabies.

Verse

Hush, my babe, lie still and slumber,
Holy angels guard thy bed.
Heav'nly blessings without number,
Gently stealing on thy head.

Hush My Baby, Lie Still, Slumber (Variation 2)

Hush my ba - by, lie still, slum - ber,

Ho - ly an - gels guard thy bed.

Heav'n - ly bless - ings with - out num - ber

Gent - ly fall - ing 'round thy head.

Verse

Hush my baby, lie still, slumber,
Holy angels guard thy bed.
Heav'nly blessings without number
Gently falling 'round thy head.

Hush My Dear, Lie Still and Slumber (Variation 3)

J.S. Bach

Hush my dear, lie still and slum - ber,

Ho - ly an - gels guard thy bed.

Heav'n - ly bless - ings with - out num - ber,

Gen - tly fall - ing on thy head.

Verse

Hush my dear, lie still and slumber,
Holy angels guard thy bed.
Heav'nly blessings without number,
Gently falling on thy head.

Hush, My Little Bird

Hush, my lit - tle bird, close your drows - y eyes,

Ey - loo - loo - loo. Rest in

peace my child, un - der star - ry skies,

Ey - loo - loo - loo. Moth - er's

al - ways near, so you need not fear,

Ey - loo - loo - loo.

Sleep and have sweet dreams, while your young life seems,

full of light and love, Ey - loo - loo - loo.

Verse

Hush, my little bird, close your drowsy eyes,
Ey-loo-loo-loo.
Rest in peace my child, under starry skies,
Ey-loo-loo-loo.
Mother's always near, so you need not fear,
Ey-loo-loo-loo.
Sleep and have sweet dreams, while your
young life seems, full of light and love,
Ey-loo-loo-loo.

I Gave My Love a Cherry (The Riddle Song)

I gave my love a cher-ry with-out a stone; I gave my love a chick-en with-out a bone; I gave my love a ring, with-out an end; I gave my love a ba-by with no cry-in'.

Verse 1

I gave my love a cherry without a stone;
I gave my love a chicken without a bone;
I gave my love a ring, without an end;
I gave my love a baby with no cryin'.

Verse 2

How can there be a cherry without a stone?
How can there be a chicken without a bone?
How can there be a ring without an end?
How can there be a baby with no cryin'?

Verse 3

A cherry when it's bloomin',
  it has no stone;
A chicken when it's peeping,
  it has no bone;
A ring when it's rolling,
  it has no end;
A baby, when he's sleeping,
  there's no cryin'.

Kumbayah *West Indian*

Refrain

Kum - ba - yah, my Lord, Kum - ba - yah,

Kum - ba - yah, my Lord, Kum - ba - yah,

Kum - ba - yah, my Lord, Kum - ba - yah,

Oh, Lord, Kum - ba - yah.

Refrain

Verse 1

Someone's crying, Lord, Kumbayah,
Someone's crying, Lord, Kumbayah,
Someone's crying, Lord, Kumbayah,
Oh, Lord, Kumbayah.

Refrain

Verse 2

Someone's singing, Lord, Kumbayah,
Someone's singing, Lord, Kumbayah,
Someone's singing, Lord, Kumbayah,
Oh, Lord, Kumbayah.

Refrain

Verse 3

Someone's sleeping, Lord, Kumbayah,
Someone's sleeping, Lord, Kumbayah,
Someone's sleeping, Lord, Kumbayah,
Oh, Lord, Kumbayah.

Refrain

La La La La

La la la la la la la la la la, La la la la la la la la la la, Ba - by's al - most sleep - ing.

Verse

La la la la la la la la la la,
La la la la la la la la la la,
Baby's almost sleeping.

substitute baby's name

Lady, Lady

Lady, La-dy, Buy a broom for my ba-by. Sweep it low, sweep it high, Sweep the cob-webs out of the sky. La-dy, La-dy, Buy a broom for my ba-by.

Verse

Lady, Lady,
Buy a broom for my baby.
Sweep it low, sweep it high,
Sweep the cobwebs out of the sky.
Lady, Lady,
Buy a broom for my baby.

Little Baby Sweetly Sleep

Lit-tle ba-by sweet-ly sleep, do not stir,

I will give a coat of fur. I will rock you,

rock you, rock you, I will rock you,

rock you, rock you. See the coat to

keep you warm, Gent-ly 'round your lit-tle form.

Verse

Little baby sweetly sleep, do not stir,
I will give a coat of fur.
I will rock you, rock you, rock you,
I will rock you, rock you, rock you.
See the coat to keep you warm,
Gently 'round your little form.

Lula, Lula, Lullaby *Israel*

Lu - la, lu - la, lull - a - by,_____

Sleep my dear lit - tle lamb._____

Lu - la, lu - la, lull - a - by,_____

Sleep my child for____ here____ I____ am.

Verse

Lula, lula, lullaby,
Sleep my dear little lamb.
Lula, lula, lullaby,
Sleep my child for here I am.

Little Red Bird of the Lonely Moor

Refrain

Lit - tle red bird of the lone - ly moor,

Lone - ly moor, lone - ly moor,

Lit - tle red bird of the lone - ly moor, O

where did you sleep in the night?

Refrain

Verse 1

Out on a gorse bush, dark and wide,
Dark and wide, dark and wide,
Swift rain was falling on every side,
O hard was my sleep last night.

Refrain

Verse 2

Did I not sleep on the swaying briar,
Swaying briar, swaying briar,
Tossing about as the wind rose higher,
O little I slept last night!

Refrain

Verse 3

Did I not sleep on the cold wave's crest,
Cold wave's crest, cold wave's crest,
Where many a man has taken his rest,
And O, my sleep was too tight.

Refrain

Los Pollitos Dicen *Spanish*

Los po - lli - tos di - cen, "Pi - o, pi - o, pi - o,"

Cuan - do tien - en ham - bre, cuan - do tien - en frí - o.

Verse 1

Los pollitos dicen, "Pio, pio, pio,"
Cuando tienen hambre,
  cuando tienen frío.

Verse 2

La gallina busca el maíz y el trigo,
Les da de comer y les busca abrigo.

Verse 3

Bajo sus dos alas, acurrucaditos,
Cuando tienen suerio,
  duermen los pollitos.

General Translation:

Verse 1
The little chicks say, "Cheep, cheep,
  cheep,"
When they are hungry and cold.
Verse 2
The hen searches for corn and
  wheat,
She goes seeking shelter,
  and feeds them grain to eat.
Verse 3
Under their wings, folded up,
When they are sleepy,
  the chicks sleep.

Pio, Pio, Pio (Variation of Los Pollitos Dicen) *Spanish*

"Pi - o, Pi - o, Pi - o," di - cen los po - lli - tos,

Cuan - do tien - en ham - bre, cuan - do tien - en frí - o.

Ba - jo sus dos a - las a - cur - ru - ca - di - tos.

Has - ta o - tro di - a, duer - men los po - lli - tos.

Verse 1

"Pio, pio, pio," dicen los pollitos,
Cuando tienen hambre,
  cuando tienen frío.
Bajo sus dos alas acurrucaditos.
Hasta otro dia, duermen los pollitos.

Verse 2

La mamá les busca,
El maíz y el trigo.
Les da la comida
Y les presta abrigo.

General Translation:

Verse 1
"Cheep, cheep, cheep," say the chicks
When they are hungry and cold.
Underneath their curled wings
Until another day, the chicks sleep.
Verse 2
Mama searches for food,
The corn and the wheat.
She gives them a meal
And lends shelter.

Lullaby, Lullaby

Lull - a - by,   lull - a - by.   Do   not wake and   weep.

Soft - ly   in   the   cra - dle lie,   sleep,   o   sleep!

Soft - ly   in   the   cra - dle lie,   sleep my dar - ling,   sleep.

Verse

Lullaby, lullaby.
Do not wake and weep.
Softly in the cradle lie, sleep, o sleep!
Softly in the cradle lie,
  sleep my darling, sleep.

Mammy Loves and Pappy Loves

Mam - my loves and Pap - py loves And

Mam - my loves her ba - by.

Go to sleep - y, go to sleep,

Go to sleep my ba - by

Verse

Mammy loves and Pappy loves
And Mammy loves her baby.
Go to sleepy, go to sleep,
Go to sleep my baby.

Naa Ska'en Liten (The Cradle Is Ready) *Norway*

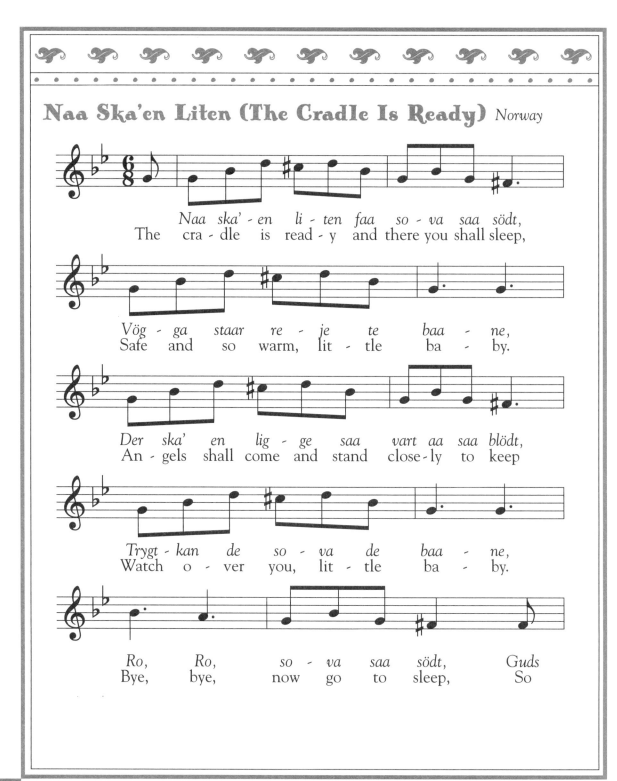

Naa ska' - en li - ten faa so - va saa södt,
The cra - dle is read - y and there you shall sleep,

Vög - ga staar re - je te baa - ne,
Safe and so warm, lit - tle ba - by.

Der ska' en lig - ge saa vart aa saa blödt,
An - gels shall come and stand close - ly to keep

Trygt - kan de so - va de baa - ne,
Watch o - ver you, lit - tle ba - by.

Ro, Ro, so - va saa södt, Guds
Bye, bye, now go to sleep, So

en - gel tar va - re paa baa - ne.
sweet - ly to sleep, lit - tle ba - by.

Verse

Naa ska'en liten faa sova saa södt,
Vögga staar reje te baane,
Der ska' en ligge saa vart aa saa blödt,
Trygtkan de sova de baane,
Ro, Ro, sova saa södt,
Guds engel tar vare paa baane.

Translation:

The cradle is ready
  and there you shall sleep,
Safe and so warm, little baby.
Angels shall come
  and stand closely to keep
Watch over you, little baby.
Bye, bye, now go to sleep,
So sweetly to sleep, little baby.

Mammy, Mammy Told Me-o

Verse

Mammy, mammy told me-o,
I'm the sweetest little baby in the country-o.
I looked in the glass and found it so,
Just as mammy told me-o.

Now the Day Is Over

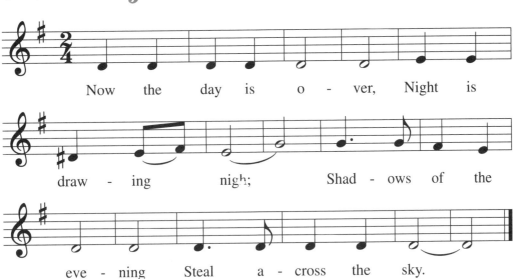

Now the day is o - ver, Night is draw - ing nigh; Shad - ows of the eve - ning Steal a - cross the sky.

Verse 1

Now the day is over,
Night is drawing nigh;
Shadows of the evening
Steal across the sky.

Verse 2

Father, give the weary
Calm and ripe repose;
With thy tender blessing,
May our eyelids close.

Oh Hush Thee, My Dove

Oh   hush thee, my dove, Oh hush thee, my row-an, Oh

hush thee, my   lap wing, My lit - tle brown bird.

Oh,   fold thy wing and seek   thy nest now, Oh,

shine   the   ber - ry   on the bright tree.   The

bird is   home from the moun - tain and val - ley, Oh

hush thee, my bird - ie, my   pret - ty dear - ie.

Verse

Oh hush thee, my dove,
Oh hush thee, my rowan,
Oh hush thee, my lap wing,
My little brown bird.
Oh hush thee, my dove,
Oh hush thee, my rowan,
Oh hush thee, my lap wing,
My little brown bird.
Oh, fold thy wing and seek thy nest now,
Oh, shine the berry on the bright tree.
The bird is home from the mountain and valley,
Oh hush thee, my birdie, my pretty dearie.

Oh, Mother Glasco

Oh, Moth-er Glas-co, where's your lamb? I left him down in the mead - ow. Birds and the bees sing-in' in the trees, Poor lit-tle lamb says, "Mam - my."

Verse

Oh, Mother Glasco, where's your lamb?
I left him down in the meadow.
Birds and the bees singin' in the trees,
Poor little lamb says, "Mammy."

Rock-a-Bye, Baby

Rock - a-bye, ba - by, on the tree top,

When the wind blows, the cra - dle will rock;

When the bough breaks, the cra - dle will fall, And

down will come ba - by, cra - dle and all.

Verse

Rock-a-bye, baby, on the tree top,
When the wind blows, the cradle will rock;
When the bough breaks, the cradle will fall,
And down will come baby, cradle and all.

Oh, Mother How Pretty the Moon Is Tonight

Oh, moth - er how pret - ty the moon is to - night, 'Twas

nev - er so pret - ty be - fore. Its

two lit - tle horns are so sharp and so bright, I

hope they don't grow an - y - more. If
I were up there with you and my friends, We'd
rock in it nice - ly you'd see. We'd
sit in the mid-dle and we'd hold by both ends, Oh,
what a nice cra - dle 'twould be.

Verse

Oh, mother how pretty
  the moon is tonight,
'Twas never so pretty before.
Its two little horns are so sharp
  and so bright,
I hope they don't grow anymore.

If I were up there with you
  and my friends,
We'd rock in it nicely you'd see.
We'd sit in the middle
  and we'd hold by both ends,
Oh, what a nice cradle 'twould be.

Rozenkes mit Mandlen (Raisins and Almonds) *Yiddish*

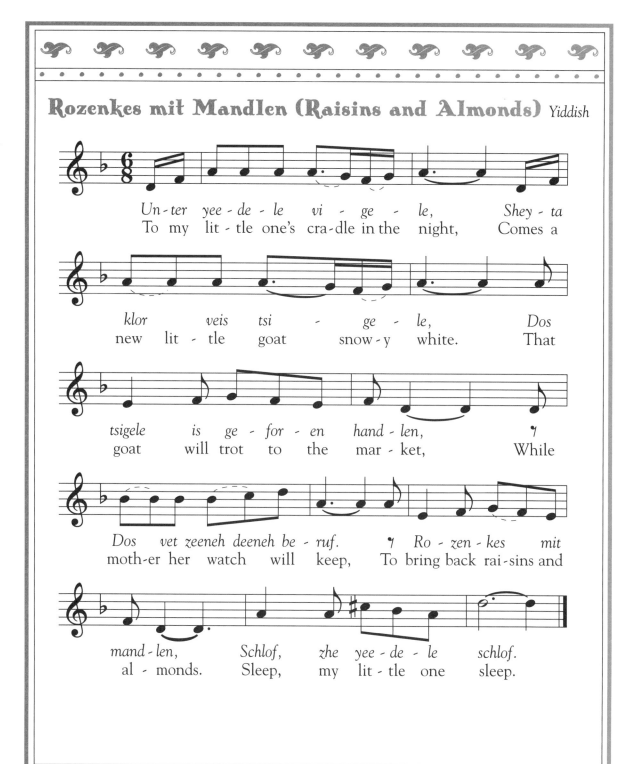

Un-ter yee-de - le vi - ge - le, Shey - ta
To my lit-tle one's cra-dle in the night, Comes a

klor veis tsi - ge - le, Dos
new lit - tle goat snow-y white. That

tsigele is ge-for - en hand - len, ⸕
goat will trot to the mar - ket, While

Dos vet zeeneh deeneh be - ruf. ⸕ Ro - zen - kes mit
moth-er her watch will keep, To bring back rai-sins and

mand - len, Schlof, zhe yee - de - le schlof.
al - monds. Sleep, my lit - tle one sleep.

Verse

Unter yeedele vigele,
Sheyta klor veis tsigele,
Dos tsigele is geforen handlen,
Dos vet zeeneh deeneh beruf.
Rozenkes mit mandlen,
Schlof, zhe yeedele schlof.

Translation:

To my little one's cradle in the night,
Comes a new little goat snowy white.
That goat will trot to the market,
While mother her watch will keep,
To bring back raisins and almonds.
Sleep, my little one sleep.

Schlaf, Kindlein, Schlaf (Sleep, Baby, Sleep) *German*

Schlaf, Kind-lein, schlaf. Der Va - ter hüt't die
Sleep, ba - by, sleep. Your fa - ther tends the

schaf. Die Mut - ter schüt - telt's Bäu - me - lein, Da
sheep. Your moth - er shakes the dream - land tree And

fällt her - ab ein Träu - me - lein. Schlaf, Kind-lein, schlaf.
down come all the dreams for thee. Sleep, ba - by, sleep.

Verse

Schlaf, Kindlein, schlaf.
Der Vater hüt't die schaf.
Die Mutter schüttelt's Bäumelein,
Da fällt herab ein Träumelein.
Schlaf, Kindlein, schlaf.

Translation:

Sleep, baby, sleep.
Your father tends the sheep.
Your mother shakes the
  dreamland tree
And down come all the
  dreams for thee.
Sleep, baby, sleep.

Shady Grove, My Little Love

Refrain

Shad - y grove, my lit-tle love; shad-y grove I know,

Shad - y grove, my lit-tle love; bound for the shad - y grove.

Refrain

Verse 1

Peaches in the summertime,
  apples in the fall,
If I can't have the one that I want,
  I won't have none at all.

Refrain

Verse 2

Fly away my blue-eyed friend,
  fly away my daisy,
Fly away my blue-eyed friend,
  you nearly drive me crazy.

Refrain

Verse 3

Wish I had a banjo strong,
  strung with golden twine,
And every time I'd pluck on it,
  I'd wish that girl were mine.

Refrain

Señora Santa Ana *Mexico*

Mexico

Se - ño - ra San - ta A - na,

Por qué llo - ra el ni - ño?

Por u - na man - za - na,

Que se le ha per - di - do.

Duér - ma - se, ni - ño, duér - ma - se ya,

Que ahi vie - ne el vie - jo, y se lo lle - va - rá.

Verse

Señora Santa Ana,
Por qué llora el niño?
Por una manzana,
Que se le ha perdido.
Señora Santa Ana,
Por qué llora el niño?
Por una manzana,
Que se le ha perdido.
Duérmase, niño, duérmase ya,
Que ahi viene el viejo, y se lo llevará.

General Translation:

Señora Santa Ana,
  why does the baby cry?
Oh, for an apple he has lost.
Hush little baby, sleep now I pray.
Here comes an old man
  to take you away.

Shosheen Sho *Scottish*

Sho-heen Sho, ba-by boy, Fa-ther's pride, moth-er's joy.

Bird-ie sleeps in the nest, Sun doth sink in the west.

Verse

Shoheen Sho, baby boy,
Father's pride, mother's joy.
Birdie sleeps in the nest,
Sun doth sink in the west.

Sleep, Bonnie Barney

Sleep, bon - nie Barn - ey be - hind the cas - tle,

By, by, by, by. Thou shalt have a

gold - en ap - ple, By, by, by, by.

Verse

Sleep, bonnie Barney behind the castle,
By, by, by, by.
Thou shalt have a golden apple,
By, by, by, by.

Sleep My Little One

Sleep my lit-tle one, sleep my lit-tle one,

Bye, bye, loo, loo. Close your drows-y eyes, close your

drows-y eyes, Bye, bye, loo, loo. Sleep my

lit-tle one, sleep my lit-tle one, Bye, bye, loo,

loo. Close your drows-y eyes, close your drows-y eyes,

Close your drows-y eyes, Bye, bye, loo, loo.

Verse

Sleep my little one, sleep my little one,
Bye, bye, loo, loo.
Close your drowsy eyes, close your drowsy eyes,
Bye, bye, loo, loo.
Sleep my little one, sleep my little one,
Bye, bye, loo, loo.
Close your drowsy eyes, close your drowsy eyes,
Close your drowsy eyes,
Bye, bye, loo, loo.

Slumber Time Is Drawing Near *Swedish*

Slum-ber time is draw-ing near, Night is gath - 'ring

'round us. Stars will all be bright and clear,

When the sand-man has found us. Dream sweet dreams the

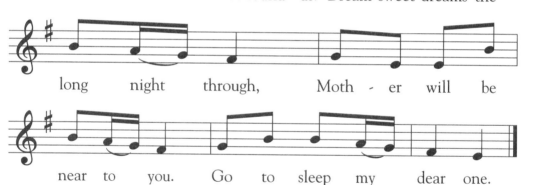

long night through, Moth - er will be

near to you. Go to sleep my dear one.

Verse

Slumber time is drawing near,
Night is gath'ring 'round us.
Stars will all be bright and clear,
When the sandman has found us.

Dream sweet dreams the long
night through,
Mother will be near to you.
Go to sleep my dear one.

The Rosebush Had a Baby

The rose - bush had a ba - by, a ti - ny wee bud. His(Her) face was white as snow. And all day she rocked him(her) to and fro To make him(her) sleep and grow.

Verse

The rosebush had a baby, a tiny wee bud.
His(Her) face was white as snow.
And all day she rocked him(her) to and fro
To make him(her) sleep and grow.

Speed, Bonnie Boat *Scottish*

Speed, bon‑nie boat, like a bird on the wing;

"On‑ward," the sail‑ors cry. Car‑ry the lad that's

born to be king Ov‑er the sea to Skye.

Loud the winds howl, loud the winds roar,

Thun‑der clouds rend the air; Baf‑fled, our foes

stand on the shore, Fol‑low, they will not dare.

Verse

Speed, bonnie boat, like a bird on the wing;
"Onward," the sailors cry.
Carry the lad that's born to be king
Over the sea to Skye.
Loud the winds howl, loud the winds roar,
Thunder clouds rend the air;
Baffled, our foes stand on the shore,
Follow, they will not dare.
Speed, bonnie boat, like a bird on the wing;
"Onward," the sailors cry.
Carry the lad that's born to be king
Over the sea to Skye.

Swing Low, Sweet Chariot

Refrain

Swing low, sweet char - i - ot,

Com - in' for to car - ry me home, Swing low, sweet

Fine

char - i - ot, Com - in' for to car - ry me home.

Verses

1. I looked o - ver Jor - dan and what did I see,
2. If you get to heav - en be - fore I do,

Com - in' for to car - ry me home, A band of an - gels
Com - in' for to car - ry me home, Tell all my friends I'm

D.C. al Fine

com - in' af - ter me, Com - in' for to car - ry me home.
com - in' there, too, Com - in' for to car - ry me home.

the book of lullabies

Refrain

Verse 1

I looked over Jordan and what did I see,
Comin' for to carry me home,
A band of angels comin' after me,
Comin' for to carry me home.

Refrain

Verse 2

If you get to heaven before I do,
Comin' for to carry me home,
Tell all my friends I'm comin' there, too,
Comin' for to carry me home.

Refrain

The Evening Is Coming

The eve-ning is com-ing, the sun sinks to rest, The

crows are all fly - ing straight home to the nest,

"Caw" says the crow as he flies o - ver-head, It's

time lit - tle peo - ple were go - ing to bed.

Verse 1

The evening is coming,
  the sun sinks to rest,
The crows are all flying
  straight home to the nest,
"Caw," says the crow
  as he flies overhead,
It's time little people were going to bed.

Verse 2

The flowers are closing,
  the daisy's asleep,
The primrose is buried
  in slumber so deep,
Closed for the night
  are the roses so red,
It's time little people were going to bed.

Verse 3

The butterfly, drowsy,
  has folded its wing,
The bees are returning,
  no more the birds sing,
Their labor is over, their nestlings are fed,
It's time little people were going to bed.

Verse 4

Goodnight, little people,
  goodnight and goodnight,
Sweet dreams to your eyelids
  'til dawning of light,
The evening has come,
  there's no more to be said,
It's time little people were going to bed.

Die Sandmännchen (The Sandman) *German, Johannes Brahms*

Die Blüme - lein sie schla - fen Schon
The flow - ers are sleep - ing Be -

längst im Mon - den - schein, Sie nick - en mit den
neath the moon's soft light, With heads close to -

Köp - fen Auf ih - ren Sten - gelein. Es
geth - er They dream through the night. And

rüt - telt sich der Blü - ten - baum, Es säu - selt wie im
leaf - y trees rock to and fro And whis - per

Traum; Schlafe, schlafe, Schlaf
low Sleep, sleep, lul - la - by, Oh

du, mein Kin - de - lein! 2.Die lein!
sleep, my dar - ling child. 2.Now child

Verse 1

Die Blümelein sie schlafen
Schon längst im Mondenschein,
Sie nicken mit den Köpfen
Auf ihren Stengelein.
Es rüttelt sich der Blütenbaum,
Es säuselt wie im Traum;
Schlafe, schlafe,
Schlaf du, mein Kindelein!

Verse 2

Die Vögelein sie sangen
So süß im Sonnenschein,
Sie sind zur Ruh gegangen
In ihre Nestchen klein.
Das Heimchen in dem Ährengrund,
Es tut allein sich kund—
Schlafe, schlafe,
Schlaf du, mein Kindelein!

Verse 3

Sandmännchen kommt geschlichen
Und guckt durchs Fenster lein,
Ob irgend noch ein Liebchen
Nicht mag zu Bette sein.
Und wo es nur ein Kindchen fand,
Streut er ihm in die Augen Sand.
Schlafe, schlafe,
Schlaf du, mein Kindelein!

Translation:

Verse 1
The flowers are sleeping
Beneath the moon's soft light,
With heads close together
They dream through the night.
And leafy trees rock to and fro
And whisper low—
Sleep, sleep, lullaby,
Oh sleep, my darling child.

Verse 2
Now birds that sang sweetly,
To greet the morning sun,
In little nests are sleeping
Now twilight has begun.
The cricket chirps its sleepy song,
Its dreamy song—
Sleep, sleep, lullaby,
Oh sleep, my darling child.

Verse 3
The Sandman comes on tiptoe
And through the window peeps,
To see if little children
Are in their beds asleep.
And when a little child he finds
Casts sand in his eyes—
Sleep, sleep, lullaby,
Oh sleep, my darling child.

Toora, Loora, Loora *Irish*

Too - ra, loo - ra, loo - ra, Oh,

too - ra, loo - ra - lie, Too - ra, loo - ra,

loo - ra, Hush now, don't you cry.

Too - ra, loo - ra, loo - ra, Oh,

too - ra, loo - ra - lie, Too - ra, loo - ra,

loo - ra, That's an I - rish lul - la - by.

Verse

Toora, loora, loora,
Oh, toora, looralie,
Toora, loora, loora,
Hush now, don't you cry.

Toora, loora, loora,
Oh, toora, looralie,
Toora, loora, loora,
That's an Irish lullaby.

Way Up High in the Cherry Tree

Way up high in the cher - ry tree, If you look,
you will see, Moth - er Ro - bin and
ba - bies three, High, high in the tree.

Fine

See the nest in the tree - tops, Swing - ing, sway - ing.

D.C. al Fine

Moth - er Ro-bin is sing-ing, Sing-ing her ba-bies to sleep.

Verse

Way up high in the cherry tree,
If you look, you will see,
Mother Robin and babies three,
High, high in the tree.
See the nest in the treetops,
Swinging, swaying.

Mother Robin is singing,
Singing her babies to sleep.
Way up high in the cherry tree,
If you look, you will see,
Mother Robin and babies three,
High, high in the tree.

Twinkle, Twinkle, Little Star *French*

A note about Twinkle, Twinkle, Little Star: Four verses of English lyrics, of which only the first verse is well-known, were first published in England in 1806. They were later set to a traditional French tune, whose original French lyrics have nothing to do with stars. We have printed all of the English verses, as well as the French lyrics that go with the tune we all know.

Twin-kle, twin-kle, lit-tle star, How I won-der what you are! Up a-bove the world so high, Like a dia-mond in the sky. Twin-kle, twin-kle, lit-tle star, How I won-der what you are!

Verse 1

Twinkle, twinkle, little star,
How I wonder what you are!
Up above the world so high,
Like a diamond in the sky.
Twinkle, twinkle, little star,
How I wonder what you are!

Verse 2

When the blazing sun is gone,
When he nothing shines upon,
Then you show your little light,
Twinkle, twinkle, all the night.
Twinkle, twinkle, little star,
How I wonder what you are!

Verse 3

Then the trav'ler in the dark
Thanks you for your tiny spark.
He could not see which way to go,
If you did not twinkle so.
Twinkle, twinkle, little star,
How I wonder what you are!

Verse 4

In the dark blue sky you keep,
Often through my curtains peep.
For you never shut your eye,
'Til the sun is in the sky.
Twinkle, twinkle, little star,
How I wonder what you are!

Original French lyrics:
Ah! Vous dirais-je, Maman,
Ce que cause mon tourment!
Papa veut que je raisonne
Comme une grande personne;
Moi je dis que les bonbons,
Valent mieux que la raison.

Translation of French:
Ah! I will tell you, Mama,
The reason for my anguish!
Papa wants me to reason like
  an adult;
But I say that candy
Is worth more than reason.

Woody, Woody, Woody, Woody

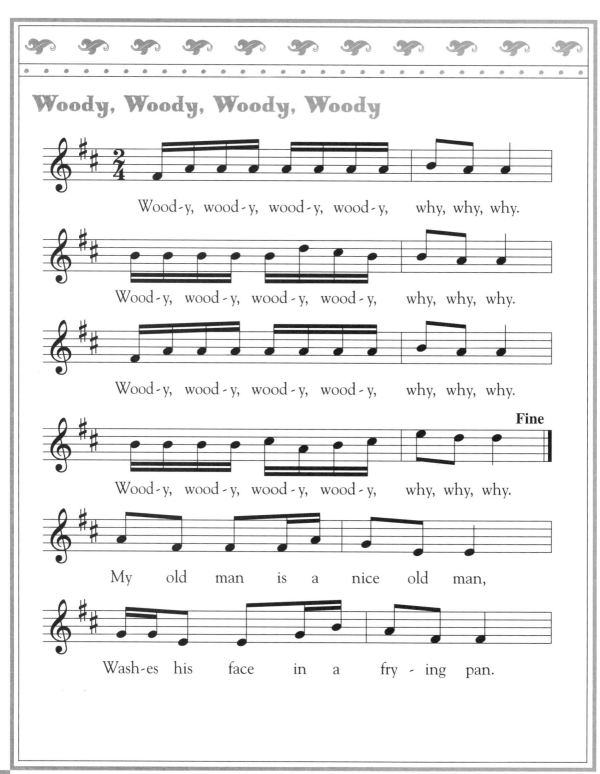

Wood-y, wood-y, wood-y, wood-y, why, why, why.

Wood-y, wood-y, wood-y, wood-y, why, why, why.

Wood-y, wood-y, wood-y, wood-y, why, why, why.

Fine

Wood-y, wood-y, wood-y, wood-y, why, why, why.

My old man is a nice old man,

Wash-es his face in a fry - ing pan.

Combs his hair with a wag - on wheel, And

D.C. al Fine

died with a tooth - ache in his heel.

Verse

Woody, woody, woody, woody, why, why, why.
Woody, woody, woody, woody, why, why, why.
Woody, woody, woody, woody, why, why, why.
Woody, woody, woody, woody, why, why, why.
My old man is a nice old man,
Washes his face in a frying pan.
Combs his hair with a wagon wheel,
And died with a toothache in his heel.
Woody, woody, woody, woody, why, why, why.
Woody, woody, woody, woody, why, why, why.
Woody, woody, woody, woody, why, why, why.
Woody, woody, woody, woody, why, why, why.

What'll We Do with the Baby?

What'-ll we do with the ba - by?

What'-ll we do with the ba - by?

What'-ll we do with the ba - by? Oh, we'll

wrap it up in cal - i - co. Wrap it up in

cal - i - co and send it to its pap - py - o.

Verse

What'll we do with the baby?
What'll we do with the baby?
What'll we do with the baby?

Oh, we'll wrap it up in calico.
Wrap it up in calico
and send it to its pappy-o.

Schlafe, Mein Prinzchen (Sleep, My Little Prince) *German*

Schla-fe, mein Prinz-chen, schlaf' ein,   Es ruhn nun Schäf-chen und Vög-e-

lein,   Gar-ten und Wie-se ver-stummt,

Ach nicht ein Bien-chen mehr summt.   Lu-na mit sil-ber-nem

Schlafe, mein Prinzchen (continued)

Schein,

Guck-et zum Fen-ster her - ein.

Schla-fe beim sil-ber-nen Schein,

Schla-fe, mein Prinz-chen, schlaf'

ein.   Schlaf' ein,

schlaf' ein.

This wonderful lullaby, composed by Wolfgang Amadeus Mozart, is included here complete with the original piano accompaniment that Mozart composed.

Verse

Schlafe, mein Prinzchen, schlaf'ein,
Es ruhn nun Schäfchen und Vögelein,
Garten und Wiese verstummt,
Ach nicht ein Bienchen mehr summt.
Luna mit silbernem Schein,
Gucket zum Fenster herein.
Schlafe beim silbernen Schein,
Schlafe, mein Prinzchen, schlaf'ein.
Schlaf'ein, schlaf'ein.

Translation:

Sleep, my little prince,
 go to sleep,
The little sheep and the little birds
 are at rest,
The garden and the meadow
 are silent,
Oh, not even a bee
 is humming anymore.
The moon has a silver glow
And looks through the window.
Sleep with the silver glow,
Sleep, my little prince, go to sleep.
Go to sleep, go to sleep.

the book of lullabies

Index by Region/Language

Index by Title